Original title:
Autumn in Verse

Copyright © 2025 Creative Arts Management OÜ
All rights reserved.

Author: Tobias Sterling
ISBN HARDBACK: 978-1-80566-680-6
ISBN PAPERBACK: 978-1-80566-965-4

A Collected Heartbeat of the Season

Leaves are falling, oh what a sight,
Twisting, turning, in pure delight.
Squirrels are laughing, they steal your nut,
While I trip over branches, oh what a rut!

Pumpkins are grinning, faces so bright,
Hiding from ghosts that give you a fright.
The air is crisp, I stole a scarf,
Worn by a statue—I'm just a laugh!

Hot cider's steaming, with a dash of spice,
Brought a friend—he said it tastes like rice.
We dance in circles, to leaves on the ground,
Oh, we're truly silly, joyful, and round!

So let's embrace this quirky time,
With laughable moments and many a rhyme.
As winter approaches, we'll gather near,
Still snickering softly, with holiday cheer!

The Timeless Cycle of Dusk

The sun is setting on a fun-filled day,
Pumpkin spice in hand, we laugh and play.
Squirrels are plotting their winter feast,
While I debate if I'm a coffee or tea beast.

Leaves tumble down like a wacky dance,
Each step we take gives nature a chance.
To crack a joke about how time flies,
As trees drop their wigs under cloudy skies.

A Symphony in Orange and Brown

The trees are dressed in their best attire,
Like fashionistas who always aspire.
Underneath them, the critters will prance,
In a game of hide and seek, they take a stance.

The wind plays tunes on branches so light,
Chasing the leaves in a comical flight.
As I trip on one, I give a loud shout,
Fall is here, that's what it's all about!

Leaves Falling Like Forgotten Dreams

In the park, kids laugh till their cheeks are red,
While I ponder over the snacks I should spread.
A leaf lands softly on my silly hat,
I swear it winked at me—how about that!

As dreams drift down like confetti of gold,
I'm gathering laughs and stories untold.
Each leaf a giggle, a secret we've shared,
In this messy world, we've all dared.

Whispering Pines and Distant Hills

The pines are whispering tales so absurd,
Of acorns wearing jackets—now that's unheard!
I grin as I stroll through the colorful scene,
Nature's hilarity is forever keen.

Boys chase the breeze, it's a wild charade,
While squirrels prepare for their nutty parade.
In this festival of fall, we all take our part,
With laughter echoing from the depths of the heart.

Shades of Rust and Earth

Leaves dance in circles, oh what a sight,
Squirrels wear acorns, such a delight.
Pumpkins grow grumpy, squished on the ground,
Giant moths bask, making a sound.

Crisp air brings sneezes, do you feel it too?
Hot cocoa's a bounty, like magic, who knew?
Sweaters are cozy, but they make you sweat,
Saying goodbye to shorts, now isn't that a pet?

Tales Woven by the Falling Light

Golden sunlight winks, a mischievous tease,
Falling down slowly, as leaves catch the breeze.
Children in piles, with laughter they roll,
Their giggles like music, that brightens the soul.

Scarecrows look puzzled, as crows fly away,
Thinking, 'Why am I dressed? It's not Halloween day!'
Cider smells sweet, like candy on lips,
But one too many sips, leads to silly slips.

Embracing the Chill of Dusk

Evenings grow longer, twilight's a hoot,
Ghost stories mingle with the chill of the fruit.
The moon sneezes softly, let's give it a laugh,
As shadows do tango, on our silly path.

Sweaters get fidgety, they itch and they tug,
While pumpkins wear grins, feeling all snug.
Bonfires spark joy, and marshmallows fly,
The laughter of friends, like stars in the sky.

The Fading Echo of Summer's Laughter

Summer waves bye, as it packs up its chair,
Waves hope you don't mind, it won't always be fair.
The sun tries to shine, but it's losing its flair,
While everyone searches for sweaters to wear.

Candies grow nutty, in wrappers they cling,
Toothbrushes shiver, they dread what we bring.
But laughter is plenty, like leaves in a clump,
As nobody cares, we just jump in the dump.

Reflections in the Puddle of October

A leaf fell down and made a splash,
My raincoat's tan turned into ash.
Puddles giggle like little kids,
Splashing all over, flipping their lids.

Squirrels dart and chase their tails,
While dodging puddles and unseen trails.
The ducks quack loud, they think they're neat,
As I stumble past them in soaked-up feet.

The Last Dance of the Sunflower

The sunflowers sway with a silly grin,
Stubbornly swaying where they have been.
They throw a ball at the passing bee,
"Come join the party, and dance with me!"

With floppy heads and seeds that drop,
They yell, "Let's party, oh, don't stop!"
As birds bring snacks, we munch with glee,
A sunflower bash, just you and me.

Nutmeg and Cinnamon in the Air

In a cozy nook, my nose picks up,
That spicy scent in a coffee cup.
Nutmeg kicks in like a cheeky chef,
While cinnamon laughs, saying, "I'm the best!"

Pumpkin parade in the kitchen room,
Spices twirling, making a zoom.
They sprinkle joy over every pie,
Whispering secrets to passersby.

Savoring the Season's End

Leaves twirl down like they're on a spree,
Kicking up colors just to tease me.
"Look at us, we're having a ball!"
As I trip over, nearly taking a fall.

The last of the cider warms my soul,
While squirrels compete for the biggest bowl.
"Who will win?" I cheer with delight,
While apples wink in the fading light.

A Tapestry of Tans and Coppers

Leaves are falling, what a mess!
Squirrels gather, in their dress.
Orange hats and red galore,
Chasing nuts, they laugh and roar.

Kites get stuck in branches high,
Breezes swirl, as kids all cry.
They're tangled in a leafy web,
As nature plays its silly ebb.

Each pumpkin's smile, a bit askew,
Scarecrows dance, a clumsy view.
The harvest moon, a laughing ball,
Winks at folks both big and small.

So bring your laughs, your silly songs,
In this season, nothing's wrong.
With every tree in vibrant sprawl,
It's a laugh-fest, after all!

The Dance of the Dwindling Day

The sun dips low, in orange cheer,
Crows in shades of black appear.
They caw and cackle, with such flair,
As shadows dance, without a care.

The wind sings tunes, a goofy strain,
Leaves swish and swirl, like they're insane.
Puddles laugh, reflecting light,
Like playful children, what a sight!

Mismatched socks on muddy feet,
Tripped by roots, we can't compete.
Laughter rings through golden fields,
As joy the very air now yields.

Fireflies twinkle, a silly show,
While the night whispers, "Let's not go."
With every giggle, dusk is fun,
In this dance, we've all just won!

Pumpkin Spice and Candlelight

Candles flicker with a flare,
Pumpkin spice is everywhere!
With every sip, a giggly grin,
Autumn's laughter now begins.

Sweaters cozy, fuzzy socks,
Time to play some silly knocks.
As pies bubble and aromas rise,
Who knew spice held such surprise?

Ghosts in sheets drift by the door,
Cackles echo, 'Is that more?'
Children shriek, 'A spooky fright!'
Yet smile at shadows in the night.

So bake and stir, let fun ignite,
In glowing warmth and candlelight.
With laughter shared, our hearts can soar,
In pumpkin dreams forevermore!

Echoes of the Gathering

Voices rise with zest and cheer,
Festival time, let's all draw near!
With apple bobbing, splashes loud,
We find delight in every crowd.

Costumes worn, a jumbled thing,
What's that? A pumpkin dressed as a king?
The funniest sight, who could resist,
As laughter swirls in a glowing mist.

Hot cocoa flows in silly mugs,
With marshmallows shaped like bugs.
We cheer for friends, so full of fun,
Joy unleashed, we're everyone!

So here we gather, warm and bright,
Chasing worries into the night.
With every chuckle that we share,
This season's magic fills the air!

Canvas of Crisp Air

Leaves dance like clowns, twirling down,
Squirrels wear acorns like tiny crowns.
Pumpkin spice lattes, oh what a treat,
But watch out for that spilled coffee on your feet!

Sweaters come out, knitted with care,
Who wore this color? I'm not quite aware.
Mittens mismatched, a fashion faux pas,
Who needs runway when nature's the star?

Fields shimmer gold, a kaleidoscope sight,
Chasing the sunset, oh what a delight.
The chill in the air insists on a sneeze,
Why's everyone laughing? It's a string of wheeze!

In this season's play, we find our part,
Giggling with friends, all merry at heart.
So take up your canvas, paint it with cheer,
For this joyful time rolls back every year!

Rhapsody of Rustling Foliage

Rustling leaves play musical tunes,
Walnut squirrels dance under the moons.
Crisp air fills lungs, a chilly embrace,
Oops, I tripped! Now I'm in lumberjack's place!

Nature's confetti, bright reds and browns,
Every step crunches like Broadway clowns.
Worn-out boots, it's a real fashion trend,
If I fall again, I'll need a good mend!

Hot cocoa's steaming in mugs full of joy,
Mugs get mistaken for each little boy.
Each sip is a giggle, each laugh a delight,
Even my dog thinks that squirrels take flight!

As twilight descends, shadows take stage,
Puns about pumpkins, oh how we engage!
Gather 'round the fire, let stories ignite,
With every chuckle, the stars shine so bright!

Twilight's Whispering Breeze

Whispers float gently on the evening air,
Woolly hats hiding hair, beware of the scare.
Bobbling pumpkins light up like a dream,
Careful on the steps, they glisten and gleam!

Breezes carry tales only the crickets know,
Beneath the harvest moon, shadows start to glow.
A giggle escapes from a little haystack,
Owls hoot a laugh, then they quietly stack!

As the dusk unfolds, laughter fills the night,
Mice in capes scurry, what a comical sight.
The chill wraps around us like a funny prank,
Let's share the warmth, or give each other a shank!

So gather your friends and toast to the way,
The nights are for laughter; let's dance and play.
This season greets us with a playful tease,
In the air-borne magic, we find our ease!

Furthering Fireside Tales

Gather 'round the fireplace crackling bright,
Telling ghost stories that give quite a fright.
The marshmallows melt—oh what a sticky mess,
S'mores with a twist, now that's a true test!

Flip-flops and heaters don't mingle too well,
Cozy socks come out, under blankets we dwell.
Neighbors peek in with a curious frown,
Wondering if we're an autumnal clown town!

Candles flicker, shadows dance on the wall,
Each tale grows wild as the night starts to crawl.
Uncle Joe's jokes never cease to astound,
We burst out with giggles that bounce all around!

So lift up your glass to this merry brigade,
With laughter and stories, our fears will soon fade.
Life is a hoot when the chill winds do blow,
Here's to fireside fun, with friends we all know!

Cloak of the Waning Light

The sun wore a frown, a quilt too tight,
A squirrel stole acorns, what a silly sight.
Leaves danced like they were at a ball,
Tripping and slipping, they'd tumble and fall.

Jackets reappear, though we sweat underneath,
Sweaters that scratch, giving us grief.
Pumpkins on porches, with faces so bright,
Thinking they're better than us every night.

The Sway of the Sorrowful Willows

Willows sway low like they're trying to peek,
Are they tipsy, or is it just the breeze streak?
They tell me secrets, but in whispers of woe,
About socks gone missing, where do they go?

Branches are lazy, like they've got a date,
But I swear they're just overthinking their fate.
The ground's a soft carpet of crunch and delight,
With oodles of shivers, but none of the fright.

Harvest Whispers

Fields boast yellow like a grand buffet,
Cornstalks are gabbing, gossiping away.
Mice throw a party, they're bold little pests,
Graffiti on pumpkins, who says they can't jest?

Baskets are full, but the pies always sneak,
Spices are dancing, with flavors unique.
The scarecrow's grinning, his job's not so bad,
With crows chit-chatting, quite the feathered fad.

Golden Leaves of Yesterday

Golden leaves whisper tales of the past,
Swirling like dancers, oh, how they can blast!
A dog runs by, snatching a prize,
An acorn, a treasure, much to his surprise.

Thoughts of winter turn heads with a chill,
But giggles escape as we leap down the hill.
Nature in flair, comical and bright,
A painting of laughter, from morning till night.

The Last Blossom of the Year

The last bloom giggles, colors so bright,
It wonders why winter's putting up a fight.
Its petals are whispering jokes to the bee,
"Catch me if you can, you'll need a cup of tea!"

The sun rolls its eyes, hiding behind a cloud,
While leaves try to dance, oh how they feel proud!
"I'll show you some moves, I'm not just a tree!"
They twirl and they flop; it's a sight to see!

The garden's a circus, with pumpkins in hats,
One pumpkin claimed, "I'm the King! How about that?"
They chuckle as critters prepare for their feast,
A march into winter, but not just the least!

With chatter and laughter, the flowers sigh slow,
As they wave goodbye, putting on a show.
They'll snooze through the frost, with dreams full of cheer,
Until springtime arrives, and blossoms appear!

When the Wind Whispers Secrets

The wind swirled in, with stories to share,
Telling trees secrets that danced in the air.
"Did you hear what the squirrel did last night?"
"He tried to steal acorns, what a silly sight!"

Leaves catch the gossip, and rustle with glee,
"Oh, did he succeed? Or got stuck in a tree?"
The wind just chuckles, fluttering around,
"He tripped on a twig, and that's how he found!"

The branches all laughed, shaking under the weight,
Of laughter that echoed, oh, it was great!
A chorus of cackles, a rustling brigade,
As the breeze spread the tales, foundations delayed.

With a whoosh and a swirl, it bids them farewell,
Visiting more, it has secrets to sell.
And the trees just sway, their laughs float on high,
Awaiting the next time their friend comes by!

Images from a Fading Dream

Once vibrant and bold, the colors start to fade,
As dreams drift away, like leaves that are laid.
"I had a bright red, but now it's a brown,
What happened to visions of wearing a crown?"

Each branch is a painter, with brushes in hand,
Creating a canvas that looks quite unplanned.
"Is that purple I see? Or just mud from the past?"
"Nope, it's just my memory, fading too fast!"

The flowers are laughing, while falling from grace,
"We're merely a joke in this autumnal race!"
But whispers of spring don't vanish that quick,
They tease with their colors, just waiting for the trick!

So they tumble and roll, like a giggling stream,
Each petal a song, a forgotten old theme.
They knock on your door, when the chill starts to bite,
Saying, "We'll be back, when everything's right!"

Ripe Moments in the Harvest

In fields full of laughter, the veggies convene,
With carrots in pajamas, a sight so serene.
"Hey, did you see the size of that jack?"
With a grin on its face, it's a colorful snack!

The corn was a gossip, its jokes always corny,
"I heard you fell over! Now, isn't that scorn-y?"
Pumpkins chuckled back, with a wide orange grin,
"Just practicing rolling; I'm training to win!"

Tomatoes were blushing, but feeling quite fine,
"Let's salsa and dance, oh, we're ripe, it's divine!"
Together they twirled, in their harvest parade,
With fruits and with veggies, their efforts displayed!

Under the moonlight, they celebrate zest,
With laughter and cheer, they all feel so blessed.
"Here's to the moments we cherish and save!"
As they winked at the farmer, who smiled and misgave!

Fields of Gold and Wisps of Mist

The pumpkins wear a sticky grin,
While squirrels dance as if to win.
The corn maze maps a route of glee,
Got lost? Just blame the bumblebee!

The hay bales hoot, a jolly jest,
As kids in wagons roll, obsessed.
A scarecrow's watch, with straw-stuffed pride,
He waves to crows who laugh and glide.

The fog rolls in, a blanket thick,
Where misty paths grow dry and slick.
In fields of gold, the laughter flies,
As nature plays its wild surprise!

So sip that cider, take a laugh,
With every chug, a goofy gaff.
For in this season, oh so bright,
Silliness takes its merry flight!

In the Wake of the Gathering Storm

The skies prepare their battle roar,
While puddles form, a great uproar!
Umbrellas flip like tiny boats,
As raindrops fall with gleeful notes.

The wind's a trickster, swirling fast,
It steals my hat, a playful blast.
Leaves twirl down like ballerinas,
In nature's show, with silly schema.

A thunderclap, a horse's neigh,
Nature's prank set on display.
We laugh and sprint to dodge the drops,
As laughter echoes, never stops!

Once the clouds retreat in peace,
We'll splash through puddles with our fleece.
For every storm's a comic joint,
Where joy and laughter will anoint!

A Mosaic of Nature's Farewell

The leaves are dressing up in flair,
With reds and golds beyond compare.
They twirl and swirl, a grand parade,
As crickets chirp a serenade.

The geese honk through their flying spree,
Like noisy kids who wish to be free.
'Til winter's chill brings hugs of snow,
But for now, let that warm wind blow!

Acorns drop with a plop and pop,
Each thunk a tickle, roofs don't stop.
The world's alive, a circus play,
With laughter echoing all the way!

So gather 'round, the show's begun,
With nature's jokes, we laugh and run.
For in these days, a whimsy blend,
Makes every moment a laugh to spend!

Beneath the Grey and Golden Sky

The clouds, they fume, a moody crew,
While golden leaves get quite the view.
They waltz along, a crunchy dance,
As kids and dogs join in their prance.

With every gust, the laughter flies,
As kites take off to silly highs.
In puddles deep, we splash and play,
While raindrops giggle on their way!

A cozy sweater, snug and tight,
We sip hot cocoa, oh what a sight!
With marshmallows that bounce and cheer,
This time of year is why we're here!

So let the grey bring mischief near,
And let the gold spark endless cheer.
For every sip and every grin,
We'll chase the season, let the fun begin!

The Timekeeper's Final Acolyte

The clock struck twelve, a little loud,
Leaves danced like they were in a crowd.
A squirrel in shades, cracking a nut,
Said time's a joke, so here we strut.

The apples rolled, they took a flight,
While pumpkins giggled, what a sight!
A merry band of jolly trees,
Challenged a breeze, 'We'll sneeze with ease!'

The acorns tumbled, giving chase,
To the wind's laugh, a frantic race.
Time slipped on, like butter on toast,
Who knew that leaves could dance the most?

With clocks confused, they laughed till late,
A silly dance, a twist of fate.
The timekeeper grinned, what a delight,
Still on the run, till the morning light.

Sketches in the Blush of Dusk

The sun went down, a painter's thrill,
In shades of pink, it paused to chill.
A crow in a beret, took to flight,
Critiqued the sky, 'It could be bright!'

Squirrels in capes, raced through the trees,
Planning a gala with the bumblebees.
With acorns in hand, they gathered round,
For woodland dance, the best in town!

A fox in boots, what a delight,
Twirled with a hare under dusky light.
'Can we start now?' the owl cried loud,
'Improvise, everyone!' cheered the crowd.

So sketches were made with giggles and spins,
As twilight waltzed with their playful grins.
In every stroke, laughter prevailed,
Nature's art show, the colors unveiled.

Lanterns in the Twilight of the Year

Lanterns flickered, oh what a charm,
Scaring away the chilly harm.
Ghosts of pumpkins hummed a tune,
Inviting all beneath the moon.

A witch on a broom, lost her way,
Sipped cocoa with ghosts, much to their play.
'You're all too kind,' she'd jokingly say,
'Could you fly with me, save my day?'

The bats in ties flitted with flair,
While owls wore glasses, quite debonair.
'Is it Halloween, or just a ruse?'
'Who cares!' laughed the trees, sipping their brews.

So lanterns glowed and laughter soared,
As creatures gathered, never bored.
In twilight's arms, they swirled as one,
A festival of joy, till the day was done.

Wistful Winds and Hidden Paths

The wind whispered secrets, quite absurd,
A tune so silly, it almost blurred.
Leaves rustled in a giggly bunch,
As nature decided to throw a brunch.

Mice in tuxedos made quite a show,
Dancing with cheese, putting on a glow.
'The cheese is ours!' they all would shout,
While cats in top hats played it out.

With every gust, a silly prank,
A leaf would tickle a tree's tall flank.
A sneaky squirrel, in search of fun,
Dared the breeze to race, just to run.

Through hidden paths where laughter lies,
Wistful winds spun tales in the skies.
In the hug of nature, giggles thrived,
A joyful world, where whimsy arrived.

Soliloquy of the Shivering Branches

The branches shake like they've seen a ghost,
Their leaves are ruffled, oh what a roast!
A squirrel's dance makes them shiver and quake,
Claiming the nuts with an acorn mistake.

The sunlight dims like a bulb on the blink,
While birds in the breeze laugh and wink.
A crow makes jokes, oh what a wise guy,
As the sun dips low in the orange sky.

They chat of the days when the sun blazed bright,
Now they wear sweaters, oh what a sight!
The wind has tickled their leafy abode,
Causing wisecracks on this humor road.

But here they jive, in their leafy attire,
With giggles of frost that never tire.
Branches may shiver, but hearts are so light,
In the cool of the dusk, what a funny sight!

The Twilight Thicket

In twilight's grasp, the shadows conspire,
To pull a prank, they never tire.
A hedgehog rolls in his spiky disguise,
While giggles of owls echo, oh how they rise!

The sneaky bushes gossip and sway,
Telling tales of the critters at play.
A raccoon dressed up in a jester's attire,
Steals snacks from the fairies, oh never tire.

The moon peeks in, with a wink so sly,
As the thicket laughs and lets out a sigh.
The chuckles of crickets join in the fun,
While the night bustling thrives, oh what a run!

So here in the thicket, with friends all around,
Laughter and giggles in every sound.
As dusk takes the stage, they jive in delight,
In the crazy embrace of the magical night!

Scent of Decomposing Dreams

In gardens where pumpkins squashed down with a thud,
The scent of decay, not just a mild dud.
Mice scurry past, in their tiny parade,
With gourmet feasts made of mold and charade.

The leaves scatter tales of rotten delight,
As the apples, once red, now play hide and fright.
A gopher's been feasting on dreams gone to rot,
While a flash of a grin from a dark, crafty knot.

The glory of rust blooms with each passing day,
A comedy of errors, what more can we say?
As the vines entangle in a twist of confound,
With giggles of mold, oh laughter is found!

So let's raise a toast to dreams of the new,
And embrace the humor that life makes askew.
For in all of the chaos, let laughter arise,
In the scent of decay, funny life we apprise!

Orchard's Bounty Ode

Come gather round for a fruit-fueled bash,
With apples that wobble and pears that splash.
The orchards are brimming with funny delights,
As bees buzz by, with their comedic flights.

The cherries are giggling, the plums sing a song,
While the tree trunks dance, oh it feels so wrong!
A raccoon in overalls tries to make change,
For acorns and fruits, oh how so strange!

The cider's a party that tickles the nose,
With spiced-up giggles from friends in repose.
While pumpkins grin widely on the orchard's stage,
Their laughs echo far, as they bask in the age.

So let's fill our baskets with joy, not despair,
With fruits that are funny, life's plenty to share!
In this orchard of laughter, we celebrate clown,
With nature's own bounty, that never wears down!

Harmonies of Hearth and Heart

The leaves are dancing, oh what a sight,
Squirrels in sweaters, such a delight!
Pumpkin spice lattes, all in a row,
We laugh as we sip, letting cares go.

Candles are glowing, flickering bright,
Ghost stories told, giving a fright.
Marshmallows roasting, the fire sings,
While we bicker over who gets wings.

Footballs are thrown, laughter in air,
Neighbors are grumpy, but we don't care!
In cozy flannels, we start to tease,
Guess who just fell into the leaves?

As daylight saves us, the humor grows,
Hot cider spills, laughter overflows!
With each little bump, each silly mistake,
The season gives gifts, and giggles we make.

In the Shadow of Waning Days

The sun is sinking, the chill starts to creep,
Beards are growing, and snorers now sleep.
Bags of candy stacked by the door,
What will they wear? Will we keep score?

Raking the leaves, squirrels on edge,
Chasing them down, I jump off the ledge!
"Trick or treat? But wait! What's that smell?"
Oh dear, it's just Dad, who slipped and fell.

Costumes are ready, a zombie parade,
One wayward teen in a ninja charade.
We all make a pact to not say a word,
But the laughter erupts, it's completely absurd!

As shadows expand, we relish the fun,
In this wacky world, we're never outdone!
Autumn unfolds with a mischievous cheer,
Where giggles abound, and friends gather near.

The Celestial Spiral of the Season

Twinkling lights in the brisk evening air,
Pumpkins all carved with mischievous flair.
The moon's just a beacon, keeping us grounded,
But boyfriend's scarecrow looks oddly floundered!

The stars start to wink like they know our game,
While cats in the night seem to feel the same.
A playful breeze sends hats flying high,
And grandma just chuckles, "Oh, my, oh my!"

Bonfire awaiting, the marshmallows brave,
Under this sky, we misbehave.
As bacon-wrapped treats dance on a stick,
We cheer for our team, despite the score's trick!

With chilly snickers and sweaters astray,
We gather together, come what may.
In this spiraled charm, laughter is found,
As we twirl in joy, with friends all around.

Embracing Silence Amidst the Leaves

In rustling whispers, the leaves softly sigh,
While critters debate, who gets to fly high?
The acorns are falling, they shake up the trees,
While children run past, shouting with glee.

Oh! Look at that cat, with a tail so grand!
How'd it get stuck? Now it needs a hand!
Nature's comedic, it surely is true,
When squirrels start planning their absolute coup!

Gathering walnuts, they dance with delight,
But one little nut's gone, out of sight!
With giggles we ponder, what could it be?
Let's just hope it's not a hoarding spree!

As laughter subsides in the calming night air,
We relish the sounds of life everywhere.
In moments of silence, humor will sprout,
For every missed joke, there's something to tout!

Whispered Promises by the Fireside

The crackle pops, a cheerful sound,
As marshmallows spin all round.
Fritz claims his stick is the best,
While I just try to get some rest.

The flames leap high, a merry show,
As shadows dance and faces glow.
A ghostly tale brings out the fright,
But Grandma snores, it's quite the sight!

With every joke, a chuckle shared,
Our silly secrets lightly aired.
The pumpkin pies all take a dive,
As we all laugh and feel alive!

A whispered promise made in jest,
That next year we'll do even best!
But for now, let's roast away,
And dream of pies on brighter days!

Beneath the Boughs of Time

Beneath the boughs where squirrels play,
I spy a nut, oh what a day!
Chasing tails, they jump and glide,
While I trip over roots, a clumsy ride.

The golden leaves like confetti fall,
As I try to catch them, one and all.
But every swirl just makes me spin,
And soon I find that I can't win!

There's laughter sharp, like cider sweet,
As we gather leaves, our little treat.
But wait! Is that a cat nearby?
We run and hide, oh me, oh my!

And when the dusk wraps like a quilt,
We laugh about the times we've spilt.
Under boughs aged yet so fine,
Memories made beneath the pine!

When Squirrels Dance in the Twilight

At twilight's edge, the squirrels prance,
With acorns tucked for a nutty dance.
They leap on branches, cheeky and spry,
While I just watch, heart in the sky.

They chatter on about their stash,
While I've misplaced my own snack flash.
A peanut falls; I bend to see,
But oops! I bump into a tree!

With furry friends doing flips and spins,
I take a tumble; it's where the fun begins.
"Hey, look at me!" I shout with glee,
But the squirrels just stare, quite unimpressed, you see!

Yet still I laugh, my heart so light,
Together we dance in fading light.
Forget the acorns; it's now a game,
Life's best shared with friends just the same!

The Palette of Dusk and Dawn

The sky's a splash of orange and red,
As I sip my cocoa, right from bed.
With every sip, I warm my soul,
And watch the sun take its daily stroll.

The geese honk loud, in perfect cheer,
While I try to dodge that falling deer.
Every tumble in nature feels like art,
Who knew clumsy could be a part?

Pumpkins grin, with faces bright,
But one little face tries to take flight.
It rolls away, oh what a sight,
A veggie race into the night!

So here's to colors that boldly blend,
And laughter found around each bend.
For in the paints of dusk and dawn,
Life's sweetest moments linger on!

Sagebrush Serenades

The leaves whisper tales of their wild, wild dance,
While squirrels prepare for a nutty romance.
A breeze plays the tunes on a rickety flute,
As pumpkins debate if they're more fruit or boot.

The sun wears a scarf like it's chilly outside,
While acorns are plotting their comical pride.
Chipmunks in suits with a top hat ask why,
As the clouds pull a prank and look like a pie.

The days grow more golden, the nights full of cheer,
As the wind tells tall stories we can't quite hear.
With every soft chuckle, a crisp leaf takes flight,
While owls wink knowingly, putting up a fight.

So gather your friends for a soaring good time,
And dance with the shadows to a whimsical mime.
As nature puts on its most playful display,
We giggle along to these sagebrush ballet.

The Lullaby of the Late Garden

In the garden, cucumbers wear hats made of dew,
While carrots are gossiping—what's new with the stew?
Bees buzzing softly, with a nap on the way,
While flowers in pajamas just dream of the day.

The zucchini twirls, with a vine-swinging grace,
And tomatoes recite their most elegant phrase.
But the worms start a riot, they want to be stars,
Over broccoli sabers and potato guitars.

As dusk falls around like a thick velvet cloak,
The onions all giggle at something they spoke.
With fireflies joining to light up the show,
The garden's alive—don't you wish you could go?

So lie on the grass and let laughter preside,
For every late bloom is a joy we'll not hide.
Let the lullabies play till the stars start to twinkle,
In this garden of giggles, our worries all crinkle.

A Palette of Gilded Days

The trees wear their crowns in shades oddly bright,
While critters exchange their scare tactics by night.
The sun plays a game of hide-and-seek fun,
Laughing 'round corners, then dashing and done.

Leaves shuffle and leap as if training for shows,
And the pumpkins are sporting some dapper new clothes.
Squirrels fill up their chests with laughter and nuts,
While skunks crack jokes that have all the right cuts.

Each sunset a splash of orange and pink,
While birds in their scarves line up to take a drink.
With laughter and breezes and everything sways,
In this canvas of quirk, we'll dance through the days.

So gather your colors, and mix them just right,
For life's in the laughter beneath soft moonlight.
Let's paint all our moments with giggles galore,
And blend in our joys with all that we adore.

Stealing Moments from the Sun

Chasing sunlight like cats in a fray,
As shadows sleep softly at the end of the day.
With a wink from the sky, all is playful and bright,
While whispers of twilight tease sensibly light.

The stars throw confetti, the moon shares a grin,
As fireflies giggle, their dances begin.
Each sip of the breeze tastes like sweet lemonade,
And laughter springs up like a mischievous jade.

We frolic through fields, not a worry in sight,
As the sun tags along, making everything bright.
With moments like candy, all sticky and sweet,
We'll juggle our joys with delightful heartbeats.

So let's steal the daylight, let fun be our guide,
With a wink and a nod, let our laughter collide.
For the world is a carousel, spinning for fun,
And we're all in this dance, stealing moments from sun.

Where Acorns and Memories Fall

Acorns tumble down like jesters,
Nature's tiny clowns, oh so bold!
Squirrels dance, they're not the best,
Chasing tails with memories untold.

Leaves begin to crisp and crack,
Whispers of the past they tell.
Crunching sounds beneath the pack,
In this comedy, we dwell.

Pumpkins spice, and cookies bake,
Goblins peek from the garden patch,
Laughter erupts with each awake,
Of mishaps that made history hatch.

So gather 'round, let stories fly,
As leaves fall down like silly hats.
With every chuckle, spirits rise,
In this season full of chitchats.

Underneath the Crisp Maple Canopy

Maples blush, they've painted dreams,
A riot of colors—what a sight!
Sweaters come out, just like beans,
Hot cocoa spills, oh what a fright!

Raking leaves becomes a game,
Who can jump the highest, oh my!
But get it wrong, you'll feel the shame,
When leafy foes make you fly.

With every gust, a leaf parade,
It tickles noses, makes you grin.
Squirrels plotting with a charade,
Gathering treasures, their big win!

So let's embrace this leafy spree,
Underneath, we laugh with glee.
As nature's jesters twirl and sway,
We celebrate in a silly way.

The Softest Breath of Change

Chilly whispers tease the air,
Tickling cheeks with frosty grace.
Goblins giggle, unaware,
Of the humor in this place.

Scarves entwined like lover's knots,
In fashion faux pas, we are rife.
Missteps from warm to cold—so hot!
It's a comedy of life!

Candles flicker with a sassy glow,
Pumpkin aromas swirl and dive.
Between laughter and pumpkin dough,
Even ghosts find ways to thrive.

So share a cup and toast the cheer,
To the frolicsome times we find here.
In every chuckle, every jump,
Is a funny little autumn romp.

Swaying Branches and Time's Embrace

Branches sway like dancers bold,
A jig with leaves as their partners.
They twirl and dip, a sight of gold,
While we cheer, our hearts grow fonder.

Pine cones tumble, dodging feet,
Nature's way of playing tricks.
With every step, our laughs repeat,
As pinecones fall like playful flicks.

Moments freeze in vibrant hues,
Captured in laughter, light, and air.
We reminisce, we make our dues,
To seasons that send time to wear.

So sway with branches, laugh a while,
As autumn's glow makes us smile.
In this playful, carefree embrace,
We find joy in every space.

Tales of the Windswept Cornfield

The corn stands tall, but feels a draft,
Their whispers giggle, nature's craft.
A scarecrow's hat flies off in glee,
As crows all chuckle, 'Come fly with me!'

A pumpkin rolls, it's found the groove,
In dance with vines, they all approve.
The farmer frowns at the sight before,
As crops declare they've fun galore!

Old roots decide to tell a joke,
While critters snicker, spinning oak.
The fields erupt with laughter loud,
Cornflakes or corn jokes, they're all proud!

But when the wind starts to fright,
The cornstalks shiver—it's chilly night.
They share a hug, a playful fright,
And bid farewell to the moonlight!

Nature's Last Embrace Before Winter

The trees are in their party clothes,
Dancing leaves, the wind bestows.
A twig sneezes, spills its gold,
While squirrels stash what trees have told.

Beneath the boughs, a chipmunk schemes,
Wishes for nuts in sunny dreams.
Neighbors chuckle, the owls agree,
'Not just fall, it's a comedy spree!'

Close to the pond, frogs set the stage,
Croaking sonnets, a watery mage.
A turtle laughs, says, "Take it slow,"
While fish jump high, putting on a show!

As frost invites a soft farewell,
The air is thick with laughter's swell.
All creatures know winter will bring,
A hibernation—a sleepy fling!

The Serenade of Melancholy

In shades of rust and burnt orange glow,
The leaves discuss their wear and woe.
A maple sighs—its branches yawn,
As sunsets tease each coming dawn.

The clouds play tag with the sun's last rays,
While crickets chirp in thoughtful ways.
A crow alights with a raucous caw,
'This season's odd, let's break the law!'

The bench is empty where lovers sat,
Now only sits a grumpy cat.
With paws crossed tight, it grumbles low,
"Where are the humans? I need a show!"

Yet in the stillness, a giggle flies,
As pumpkins grin beneath cloudy skies.
Melancholy, with a cheeky twist,
In nature's arms, we still exist!

Paths Traced by Fallen Leaves

The earth wears a carpet of colors bright,
As leaves conspire to take a flight.
On every path, a crunch and crack,
While woodland critters plan their snack.

A squirrel juggles acorns with flair,
While chasing shadows without a care.
The leaves just giggle, taunting the breeze,
"Catch us if you can, if you please!"

A dog leaps high, chasing its tail,
It skids on crisp leaves—oh, what a fail!
With laughter ringing through the trees,
A small bird tweets, "Oh, yes, please!"

As evening falls and shadows stretch out,
The leaves dance to a silent shout.
In nature's jest, a playful spree,
Paths drawn by leaves, so wild and free!

Whispers of Falling Leaves

Leaves chatting loudly, what a show,
Dancing in the wind, they always glow.
A squirrel in a cap, so dapper, so spry,
Steals a shiny acorn, oh my, oh my!

Raking them up is such a chore,
But watch them fly back, oh what a score!
The trees gossip tales in rustling tone,
While we scratch our heads, feeling overgrown.

Harvest Moon Serenade

Under a moon that's big as a pie,
We gather for snacks, oh me, oh my!
Corn on the cob, buttered just right,
A raccoon steals dinner; what a sight!

Pumpkin spice lattes cheer us so bright,
But spill on your shirt? A comical plight!
Friends in plaid shirts twirl around the field,
Chasing each other like chaos revealed.

Ember Serenade

Crackling flames jump with a shout,
Who knew marshmallows would pout?
S'mores are sticky, and laughter is loud,
As a dog steals dessert, making us proud!

Blankets wrapped tight like burritos we are,
Telling ghost stories beneath a bright star.
"Was that a howl or just a loud cat?"
We guffaw together and leave it at that.

The Golden Canopy

Golden leaves shimmer, a treasure trove,
Kids leap in piles they eagerly strove.
A dad with a rake, seriously stressed,
Gets buried in laughter; a leaf pile quest!

Squirrels are ninjas, they leap with grace,
While dogs chase their tails, a comical race.
The sun sets with giggles, brightening the night,
As nature unravels its colorful light.

Nostalgia in a Faded Palette

Leaves fall down, like paper planes,
Spinning round in joyful games.
Once bright colors, now a tease,
Whispering tales of sneezes and wheeze.

Squirrels hide their acorn stash,
In a frenzy, all in a dash.
They chirp and chatter, quite absurd,
While we note down every word.

Pumpkins grin with toothy scowls,
Marked up faces, silly prowls.
Giggling kids in costumes roam,
Through streets that feel just like a tome.

So we laugh at the quirks that greet,
With every crunch beneath our feet.
Time rolls on with a quirky flair,
This season knows how to make us stare.

Silent Frosted Mornings

Frosty grass, the ground's a sheet,
Like nature's quilt for chilly feet.
We sip our coffee, barely wise,
As ice creeps up, and our hair defies.

Trees wear coats of silver sheen,
'Tis a look they've long unseen.
Birds debate on empty branches,
About winter coats and fancy ranches.

Puffs of breath become our dance,
In this chilly morning trance.
Who knew a sneeze could sound so loud?
As we jest, and the neighbors crowd.

Hats pulled down, we laugh and frown,
With every slip on frosty ground.
Winter's here, the jokes we share,
Make icy mornings quite the affair.

When the Sun Starts to Stretch

Sunrise paints a golden sweep,
As lazy hours reclaim their leap.
Coffee cups raise an early cheer,
For sleepy heads and dreams unclear.

Pajama squirrels take to the trees,
Chasing shadows on a tease.
Chasing tails and bouncing high,
While we wonder who's the sly.

Baked goods warm the breezy air,
With pumpkin spice beyond compare.
We sprinkle laughter on each slice,
While counting all our mischief thrice.

As days fade with a playful wink,
We toast to moments, sip and think.
When the sun stretches wide and bright,
We linger on, 'til comes the night!

The Melancholy of Migration

Birds in formation take to flight,
With honks and squabbles, quite a sight.
They argue over who's in charge,
While a lone goose thinks it's too large.

Leaves gather round in swirling dance,
Rustling plans in a haphazard prance.
Some want to stay, some want to roam,
While crows caw loudly about their home.

Nature's rush, a hurried stage,
As critters scramble to turn the page.
In cozy burrows, we need to stash,
Nibbling snacks in a frantic dash.

But while we grumble, let's not despair,
For all this chaos brings us flair.
Migration's song is loud and clear,
To find some joy in this time of year!

A Tapestry of Fallen Colors

Leaves are dancing like a jester,
Spinning down, a vibrant bluster.
Squirrels stash acorns, plotting schemes,
While I trip over roots, not as it seems.

Pumpkins wink with silly grins,
Wearing hats made from last week's sins.
Nature's palette, a playful show,
Who knew fall could steal the glow?

The Chill of Evening Light

Sweaters come out, a cozy sight,
Though I find one that's two sizes tight.
Hot cocoa spills, my fate is sealed,
Against the chill, I'm far from healed.

Ghosts of warmth keep me in fright,
While my nose turns red, oh what a plight!
Jack Frost nips at my frozen toes,
As I stumble home in clownish clothes.

Echoes of a Dimming Sun

The sun sets low, its gold tones fade,
While I chase shadows, a comical parade.
Crickets chirp their evening tune,
While I look up, wondering 'who's that moon?'

Twilight whispers, the air grows thick,
I trip on leaves, my shoelace a trick.
With every step I laugh and play,
The night is young, I'm here to stay.

Harvest Moon Serenade

The moon looks down in bright disgrace,
As I dance awkwardly, lost in space.
Cider flows, a sweet delight,
Yet I spill it like a clumsy knight.

Bonfire crackles, I sing off-key,
Friends in stitches, oh look at me!
Squash and corn make quite the spread,
If only my dance moves could be led.

The Lure of the Golden Hour

The sun is a pumpkin, round and bright,
It rolls down the sky, a funny sight.
Squirrels in suits hold a tiny parade,
Hoping for snacks that they don't have made.

Leaves do a dance in the chilly breeze,
They twirl like dancers, oh, if you please!
Waving goodbye, they fall with a grin,
'Time to drop in for a nutty spin!'

The shadows grow long, like stretching cats,
They chase after light, wearing silly hats.
Glowing with laughter, the dusk starts to play,
Whispering secrets at the end of the day.

A cozy warm drink, with marshmallows high,
Completes this odd dance 'neath the painted sky.
With giggles and chuckles, we nestle all near,
In this golden hour, there's nothing to fear!

Threads of Gold in the Fabric of Time

Stitching together the days gone by,
With needles of sunlight that pierce the sky.
Funny little critters all come to the seam,
Dancing 'round threads of a whimsical dream.

A tapestry woven with laughs and some tears,
Colors bursting forth from the fabric of years.
Gems from the harvest, so shiny and bright,
Jokingly twinkling as day turns to night.

Each thread is a story, a giggle, a glance,
In the quirk of it all, let's give life a chance.
Crafted from moments that wriggle and squirm,
Time's fickle fabric makes us each a worm.

So let's pull a thread, unravel a tale,
Where pumpkins all giggle and bumble down the trail.
In this golden patch of the passing of time,
We'll wrap up in laughter, all chunky and prime!

Memories Wrapped in Woolen Scarves

Bundled up tight in my fluffiest wear,
I trudge through the puddles, without a care.
Socks in my boots start a ticklish game,
Each step is a laugh, oh, who is to blame?

A scarf of bright colors, a festive delight,
It dances around me, what a funny sight!
Knitted with stories from seasons ago,
It whispers of snowflakes and warm cocoa flow.

Buttons all jingle like bells from the past,
They chime in the wind, oh, they're the best cast!
Wool wraps me warmly, a hug from a friend,
As laughter and joy seem to blend without end.

We twirl in the park, as leaves start to fall,
Creating a whirlwind, a chuckle-filled call.
Wrapped in this fabric, both timeless and grand,
Memories linger, as soft as the strand!

Skies Weeping the Colors of Change

The skies are a canvas, vibrant and bold,
With splashes of crimson and orange, behold!
Clouds squeeze out colors, giggling with glee,
They tickle the trees, who all sway with esprit.

Each drop is a laugh, a watercolor tease,
Dripping with joy, 'neath the shaking trees.
Puddles reflect all the wacky delight,
Squishy shoes marching, oh, what a sight!

Like nature's confetti, the leaves take a dive,
Spinning through branches, so glad to be alive.
A circle of giggles, they gather in heaps,
Crackling and crunching, in a blanket of heaps.

So here's to the skies, with their funny old ways,
Turning each moment into vibrant displays.
With giggles and joy, we dance in the rain,
As colors cascade, bringing laughter again!

A Symphony of Harvest

The pumpkins round, they start to grin,
With cornstalks dancing in the wind.
Turkeys strut with feathery pride,
While apples tumble, none can hide.

Cider flows like stories told,
Of Halloween frights and candy gold.
Squirrels stash away their loot,
While we wear sweaters, oh so cute!

Leaves fall down, a crunchy parade,
With every step, a fruit-flavored cascade.
Neighbors shout, it's time for cheer,
As we brace for the frost, oh dear!

So grab your hat and dance around,
In nature's laughter, joy is found.
With every bite of pumpkin pie,
We toast to fall without a sigh.

Firelight Reflections

The nights grow long, the fire is bright,
As marshmallows roast under starlight.
Old stories shared with laughter and glee,
While raccoons plot, oh what a spree!

We sip hot cocoa, our cheeks aglow,
The flicker of flames, putting on a show.
Chasing shadows, we jump in fright,
As leaves rustle softly, an autumn night.

We wear socks with holes and giggle aloud,
As we tell ghost stories, not too proud.
But who could be scared with chocolate nearby?
Feasting on sweets beneath the sky.

So gather close, the chill is real,
With warmth and friendship, let's make a deal.
No tricks tonight, just treats to share,
In cozy corners, sparks fill the air.

The Quieting of the World

The world slows down, it's time to play,
As the leaves turn colors, bold and gay.
Squirrels chatter about their stash,
While bunnies hop, a fluffy dash.

The winds whisper secrets to the trees,
While kids leap in piles of leaves with ease.
School buses rumble with sleepyheads,
And coffee brews as the country spreads.

The sweaters come out, snug and tight,
As we gather 'round, oh what delight!
With laughter echoing, joy in the air,
We sip and snack without a care.

As twilight falls, the stars appear,
With pumpkin spice thoughts that we hold dear.
Each moment savored, treasures amassed,
In this quiet time, we breathe deep and laugh.

Pile of Memories in the Meadow

A meadow glows with golden light,
As children play from dawn till night.
With kites that soar, and laughter loud,
We claim our space, all feeling proud.

The wind carries whispers of days gone by,
Of silly pranks and pie in the sky.
Leaves make a rustle, a soft ballet,
With every gust, the games we play.

Old boots stomp in puddles wide,
While puddles pretty much take it in stride.
As memories pile, like leaves in the field,
The joy of the moment, forever revealed.

So come and join, let's dance in the sun,
With hearts like children, we'll never be done.
Each giggle collected, like acorns so bright,
In the pile of our memories, pure delight.

A Dance of Shadows in the Grove

In the grove where shadows sway,
Squirrels dance at break of day.
Leaves are falling, taking flight,
Chasing each other, oh what a sight!

The sun peeks through with golden beams,
While ants march on with their silly schemes.
Frogs croak tunes, their chorus quite loud,
As mushrooms sprout, they feel so proud!

A fox prances, donning a cap,
While hefty bears take a cozy nap.
Laughter echoes from the deer,
As they play tag without any fear!

Twirling branches, a leafy show,
Even the owls join in the flow.
Nature giggles, can you hear?
In this grove, there's nothing to fear!

Hues of Decay

Colors fade with a comical twist,
With red and gold, how can we resist?
Pumpkins grinning, they pout in a row,
While squirrels giggle and steal the show!

Cider spills all over the grass,
As bees buzz by, they're quite a class.
The scarecrow dances, barely in place,
While crows throw peanuts, oh what a race!

With crunchy leaves beneath our feet,
The crunching sounds can't be beat.
So let's enjoy this silly spree,
Before we fade like the old oak tree!

As laughter echoes through the fields,
Nature spreads its wacky shields.
Here's to colors, joy, and cheer,
In every shade, let's give a cheer!

Beauty Remains

Beauty lingers in vibrant hues,
While critters flaunt their wacky shoes.
Chirpy birds with silly hats,
Laughing loudly at roaming cats!

Sunset throws confetti in the sky,
As rabbits hop, oh me, oh my!
A hedgehog rolls, a stylish sight,
Claiming his crown in the fading light!

Wind whispers secrets, giggling too,
As branches tickle, "Hey, howdy-do!"
With every leaf, with every sound,
The joy of cheerfulness abounds!

Let's toast to this wonderful stage,
Where laughter dances, uncaged.
Embrace the charm that still remains,
In this land of joyful refrains!

The Quiet Song of Rustling Leaves

Rustling leaves weave a funny tune,
They whisper jokes beneath the moon.
Dancing gently, they twirl and twist,
In a playful game, they can't resist!

Squirrels giggle, with nuts in tow,
Juggling acorns, putting on a show.
A chipmunk joins, strutting with flair,
While a raccoon shimmies without a care!

The breeze chuckles, a mischief in its play,
As the trees sway in a silly ballet.
Branches reach out, in a poking game,
Tickling the folks who walk the same!

So hum along to nature's song,
Where goofiness is where we belong.
In every rustle, in every smile,
Nature's humor makes it all worthwhile!

As the World Turns to Ember

The world is blushing, quite a sight,
With twinkling stars laughing at night.
Flaming leaves giggle in the air,
Winking at the moon with a cheeky glare!

Fireflies dance like little jokes,
Glowing bright as they tease the folks.
Laughter rings from tree to tree,
While crickets chirp in harmony!

As pumpkins chuckle in front of doors,
And owls hoot from the high-up floors,
The air's alive with whimsy and cheer,
As nighttime blossoms, it becomes more clear!

So let's embrace this vibrant glow,
With giggles and joy, let's all let go.
As the world turns into a warm ember,
Let's cherish the laughter, remember, remember!

www.ingramcontent.com/pod-product-compliance
Lightning Source LLC
Chambersburg PA
CBHW071830160426
43209CB00003B/271